BY
TERRY DEARY

Kingfisher

NEW YORK

KINGFISHER
Larousse Kingfisher Chambers Inc.
95 Madison Avenue
New York, New York 10016

First edition 1996
10 9 8 7 6 5 4 3 2 1
Copyright © Larousse plc 1996
Text copyright © Terry Deary 1996

LIBRARY OF CONGRESS CATALOGING-IN-PUBLICATION DATA
Deary, Terry,
    Alien Landing/Terry Deary.
        p. cm.—(Classified)
    Summary: Examines the high-profile incident in New Mexico in 1947
which some interpret as the crash of an unidentified flying object.
    1. Unidentified flying objects—Sighting and encounters—New
Mexico—Roswell—Juvenile literature.
[1. Unidentified flying objects.]
I. Title. II. Series.
TL789.3.D425 1996 001.9'42'09789—dc20.
96–181 CIP AC

ISBN 0-7534-5004-6
Printed in Great Britain

NOTE TO THE READER

You will have to make your own minds up about how many of the "facts"
contained in this story are true. Some are based on public information, but
others are the result of a fictional interpretation by the author of events—what
might have been said or done. Some names have been changed, as you can see,
to protect the individuals involved.

CONTENTS PAGE

INTRODUCTION

Look up at the night sky on a clear evening and you will be able to see universe in all its glory—an unfathomable expanse of space dotted with a million stars. But could there be anybody else out there looking back at us?

Dreamers said there must be other life forms somewhere in the universe. We cannot be the only intelligent beings. Some scientists mocked the dreamers. They said that the Earth is unique, and the odds against a similar planet generating intelligent life are impossibly huge. They claimed that in our vast galaxy, which is a hundred thousand light years wide, they had never found a planet even remotely like ours—in fact, they have never been able to see another planet outside the solar system.

Then in 1995, scientists found a star that is very much like our Sun. It's called 51 Peg in the constellation of Pegasus. It's just 40 light years away (around 235 trillion miles)—so close that we can see it from Earth. But the exciting thing is that it has at least one planet circling it. A planet that might be capable of sustaining life. Alien life, it's true, but other beings all the same.

Those beings might be three to five billion years older than humans.

And, if we can see them, then they can certainly see us. And if we Earthlings dream of sailing to the stars, then maybe they're curious about us too. And if they're billions of years older and wiser than us, then maybe they have the power to reach Earth.

A British astrophysics professor argued, "It may well be that we are alone after all. If beings on 51 Peg have had a three to five-billion-year start on us then you'd imagine that they'd be here by now."

The professor is right, of course. They would be here by now.

But perhaps they are.

Perhaps they've arrived. Perhaps they arrived here before humans. Maybe humans have seen them from time to time. Possibly they are the gods of myth and legend, or the miraculous lights that sometimes appear in the sky.

Is there any evidence that they have arrived? Perhaps.

Where is this evidence?

Locked away in secret government files. Files that most people never get to see.

Files marked:

CHAPTER ONE

"No one leaves the FBI," my chief said. "Well, not unless it's in a wooden box. Do you understand what I'm saying?"

"Yes, sir," I said. My voice didn't quite come out the way I meant it—the tension had made my throat swell. Either that or my shirt collar had shrunk with the sweat.

He kept me standing in front of his desk while he sat back and looked at the screen of his laptop computer. At last he said, "You've been with us a year now, Rod. A sort of probation. You've followed experienced agents in the field and contributed to a variety of investigations. As far as we're concerned your work has been satisfactory." He squinted at the screen. "Exemplary, in fact."

"Thank you, sir."

I waited. Was he going to come up with some "but" that would send me back to the police force that I'd joined after college? After a year with the FBI the police seemed suddenly mundane. Ordinary. I felt sweat trickle down my forehead into my right eye and murmured a prayer to myself: "Please don't let him say, 'But'."

He said, "But..." and my heart sank. "You have to decide if you are prepared to sacrifice a normal life to become a full-fledged agent."

"Me?" I said and tried to get my brain around what he was saying. He was offering me the job if I was prepared to take it. Prepared to take it? I'd swim the Pacific to get that job!

"Yes," he said calmly. "Once you join you will have access to state secrets. Secrets that no one outside the FBI, except the President himself, will ever know.

classified information. You can't retire from the FBI and hand that information back when you hand in your gun and your badge. The information stays in your head and you are bound by oath to keep it there."

I straightened my back, "Yes, sir."

"That's not something you undertake lightly," he went on. "No gossiping, no selling stories to the media... though some of them would be worth a fortune!" His voice was soft but the words were about as gentle as a scalpel. "The FBI does not take kindly to someone who retires, then talks about their classified assignments."

"No, sir." I swallowed.

"You're young. I know retirement seems a million years away right now. But one day you'll be glad I warned you about this. One day you'll be old. You'll be sitting by the fire with your mind full of memories, and you'll want to share them. Your oath will stop you. Even when in years to come case files you helped put together are opened, you won't be allowed to discuss them."

"I understand."

He looked up thoughtfully. "I want you to do just one thing for me before you take that oath. Before you commit yourself to the Bureau for the rest of your life. I want you to talk to a retired agent."

"Sir?"

"In his day he was one of the best. In his head is one of the most amazing stories you'll ever hear. It's about one particular case he worked on. Most of the files on it have been opened over the past few years, and the vultures have been trying to get his story out of him and make it front page news. But this agent still refuses to talk."

He continued, "I won't tell you his name, but I'll tell you his story. Let's just call him Agent Smith. John Smith. Talk to him and see if you think you can be as loyal, as committed as he was. As he still *is*. Do you understand?"

"Yes, sir."

He nodded his head slowly and his glasses caught the yellow light of the lamp on his desk. Then he hit me with a question that I wasn't expecting.

"What do you know about flying saucers, Rod?"

I tried not to laugh. It was a serious question and I had to take it straight. "So-called 'flying saucers' are alien spacecraft. The term was first coined in the summer of 1947 after an airplane pilot named Ken Arnold reported seeing nine bright objects in the sky near Mount Rainier, Washington. He said they were boomerang-shaped but they skimmed along like saucers on the surface of the lake. One of the reporters, Bill Bequette, picked up on that and called them 'flying saucers.' The name kind of stuck."

He nodded. "You know a lot."

"My hobby is surfing the Internet, sir," I said.

He glanced down at the computer screen and allowed himself a smile. "I know."

Of course he knew. Not only did an agent keep the Bureau's secrets—the Bureau kept all the agent's secrets. "There are a lot of people who use the Internet to exchange information on UFOs...flying saucers, alien abductions, that sort of thing," I said.

His eyes were steady behind the glasses, watching me like a snake watches a frog, waiting to see which way I would jump. "So, you'll be familiar with the incident at Roswell?" he said quietly.

I tried to keep my face neutral, impassive, the way I'd been trained to. "Yes, sir." My memory was one of my strengths. I could close my eyes and recall pages of information. "On July 2, 1947, a rancher named Mac Brazel was at home in Corona, New Mexico. He heard an explosion and saw something red with a white tail fall to the Earth up in the hills."

3

"There was a thunderstorm at the time," the Chief pointed out. "It could have been ball lightning." He seemed to be trying to test me out.

"Sure," I said. "But a couple of days later, when he was driving some sheep out, he came across what appeared to be wreckage. Strange pieces of silver foil. He picked up a few bits of metal and took them to his neighbors, the Proctors. They found that the foil was so strong that it couldn't be cut or burned. They figured it had to be part of an alien spacecraft."

"Of course." He smiled. "There'd been two weeks of nonstop reports in the newspapers about mysterious lights in the sky. Everyone was talking about flying saucers. People were seeing them under the bed! It's a mental condition known as hysteria!"

"I agree," I said. "But there *might* have been some genuine reports in the middle of all those phoney ones. Anyway, the Proctors told Mac Brazel that he should claim the $3,000 reward the newspapers were offering for proof that UFOs exist."

"Plenty of people will murder for money—Mac Brazel would almost certainly tell lies about flying saucers to get a share of that $3,000," the Chief pointed out.

"But he stored some of that wreckage and then called in the army to investigate," I said slowly, desperately trying to dredge the details from my memory.

"No-o..." the Chief told me. He punched a few keys on the keyboard. A rainbow of screen colors reflected on his face as he scanned the screen intently. "Mac Brazel called in the sheriff. Sheriff George A. Wilcox. It was the sheriff who called in the military."

I began to remember. "You're right. It *was* the sheriff who called the military, and they turned up soon after he put the phone down...too soon. It's almost as if they were expecting a call. As if they knew something had crashed but were waiting to find out where."

"Yes!" he agreed. "A Colonel William Blanchard was a commander at the local air base at Roswell. He had a military intelligence officer named Major Jesse Marcel with him...oh, and all the subsequent investigations mention some guy in civilian clothes. A counter-intelligence agent."

"I don't remember his name," I said slowly.

The Chief allowed himself a brief grin. "No, you wouldn't. We don't usually go around announcing our names in six-foot neon lights."

I picked up on one word. "*Our*? You mean he was FBI?"

The chief nodded. "He was in the Counter Intelligence Corps attached to the army, but he was working closely with us on this case. In fact, when the CIC folded he joined us. Became one of our best agents."

Then things slipped into place like the last pieces of a jigsaw. "And this CIC agent...the one who was present at Roswell? This is the man you want me to talk to? You want me to meet John Smith?"

"First thing tomorrow." The Chief quickly keyed in a message and punched some keys to send it to a printer at the side of his desk. He slid the printed letter out, signed it, and passed it over to me. "Show him this letter. Then he'll talk to you. He'll tell you things he's been keeping to himself for 50 years. Talk to him. Try to get to know him —learn how he thinks. Find out how he deals with secrets. How he has managed to keep so much to himself all these years. Then come back here next week and answer one question. I want you to tell me whether you could keep a secret like the one John Smith has kept. If the answer is 'yes' then you can start calling yourself Agent Rod Morgan."

"And if the answer is 'no'?" I asked.

"Then I misjudged you," he shrugged. He rose slowly

and clasped my hand in his strong grip. "Good luck Rod—don't let me down."

CHAPTER TWO

I walked down the corridor and past the reception desk where a secretary was guarding the fileroom like a dragon. "Good afternoon," I said brightly.

She gazed back with cool, gray eyes and said "Good afternoon," in a toneless voice. I was on a high, knowing that within a week I'd be an agent. I'd soon have access to the millions of documents on the rows of shelving behind that fileroom door.

I went straight back to my apartment and packed. Agent Smith lived a six-hour flight away in New York City. I turned my computer on and looked up the flight times and hotel accommodation in New York. I had no problem booking the hotel but the flight was another story. It was the weekend and nothing was available until shortly before midnight. I tried suggesting it was government business but no luck. I'd just have to wait.

After packing, I still had three hours before I was due to leave. So I decided to take a short refresher course on Roswell. I threw my bag into the corner of the room and turned back to the computer.

The problem with the Internet was that there was just too much stuff on the Roswell Incident. There was a new movie due out with a fictional look at the facts and there was also talk of another supposedly authentic film that had recently been discovered. It was due to be released soon and everyone on the Internet was speculating wildly about it.

Finally I found some basic background information and downloaded it onto my screen.

It seems that Mac Brazel, the Military Intelligence Major Jesse Marcel, and Agent Smith went out to look at the site the next day. Even after 50 years nobody knows exactly who Agent Smith really was.

I made a note. John Smith must have visited the site for the first time on July 7, 1947. The three men found the wreckage scattered over a stretch of scrub land over a mile long and 300 feet wide. There was also a scar in the ground where they guessed the craft had struck before it disintegrated.

Of those three men, the rancher, Brazel, had died in the 1960s. Major Jesse Marcel had died too, but a few years before his death he had blown the whole story to some UFO investigators. I jotted down parts of Marcel's statement:

When we arrived at the crash site it was amazing to see the vast area it covered. It obviously hadn't exploded on the ground. It was something that must have exploded above the ground while traveling at a high speed. It was quite obvious to me from my experience with air activities that this was not a weather balloon, nor was it an airplane or a missile. What it was, we didn't know. We just picked up the fragments.

Then Marcel went on to say they'd found lightweight beams that had strange lettering painted on the side of them that no one could understand.

"Not Russian," he said later. "Something alien."

I figured he was just guessing. Here was some guy getting masses of public attention in his retirement. He might easily have invented tasty morsels of story to keep the media on his doorstep. It was this sort of temptation that my chief had talked about. Besides, his story didn't quite ring true. If the craft exploded above the ground, why did the three men find scars in the earth at the wreckage site, where something had crashed at a great speed? It seems that Major Marcel may have embellished his story to keep the press interested.

What about the guy who *didn't* want publicity? What would John Smith say when I talked to him? Suddenly I was impatient to get to New York. But I still had over two hours to wait. I turned back to Major Jesse Marcel's statement:

A lot of the wreckage was little beams with symbols on them. We had to call the symbols hieroglyphics because I couldn't interpret them and they couldn't be read. But they must have meant something. They weren't all the same either. They were a sort of pinkish-purple color—I suppose you'd call it lavender. I tried to burn the paint off the symbols, but they wouldn't burn any more than the alloy metal of the beams themselves.

I skimmed the report and read on:

But what's even more astounding is that the piece of metal that we brought back was so thin, just like the tinfoil in a pack of cigarettes. I didn't think anything of it at first, then someone came to me and said, "You know that metal there? I tried to bend the stuff and it won't bend. I even tried hitting it with a sledge hammer. You can't make a dent in it. And it's so light it weighs practically nothing." I didn't actually see him hit it with a sledge hammer but he was a very honest, truthful sort of guy. I believed him. Like I said before, I knew quite a bit about the materials used in airplanes, but this was like nothing I had seen before. Even now, I still don't know what it was.

Impressive, I thought. Some of the reports I read said that other sheets of foil from the wreckage could be crumpled up for hours. But as soon as you let it go, the stuff straightened itself out to exactly the same shape it was before. Not a mark, not a crease. What sort of material could do that? We hadn't invented such stuff even 40 years later!

Major Marcel and Agent Smith knew they had something strange. They loaded some of the debris into Marcel's 1942 Buick and took it back to Roswell Air Base. Next morning Major Blanchard ordered that the site be sealed off...that made sense. It wouldn't do for a story like that to break out before the government had time to thoroughly examine the evidence. The military also decided that Brazel should be brought in. Best to be on the safe side. This was all good FBI practice, and I nodded my approval at the screen.

Then something out of place made me sit up. The air base issued a press release. At first I assumed they were going to deny that anything had ever landed, but they issued a press statement saying that they'd found a flying saucer and they'd taken it in for examination! I blinked and read it twice:

The many rumors regarding flying disks became reality yesterday. A crashed alien ship was recovered near Roswell and taken to the air base in the town...

What sort of idiot sent that out! Must have been some junior press officer. A statement like that would only cause panic and confusion on a grand scale—making it impossible for our guys to do their job. And how did Agent John Smith react? I made a note to ask him.

The reaction of the media had been predictable. There were phone calls to the sheriff from all over the world! Reporters flocked to Roswell in droves. Hardly surprising.

That press release was one lousy idea. Somebody would have a lot of explaining to do.

I grabbed my bag and my notes and headed for the airport.

CHAPTER THREE

The stuffy airport lounge seemed suffocating after the cold air outside. Announcers canceled flights, babies cried, and tired families shouted at each other. I didn't envy them. I was planning to marry the FBI.

During the next six hours on the flight I sorted out the details of the Roswell Incident, piecing together the stories of the witnesses and the investigators who came along later.

July 8, 1947 was an interesting day at Roswell. It started with that press release—"A crashed alien ship was recovered!" Local papers printed the story, and local radio started to broadcast it.

Then suddenly the story changed. "An alien ship has NOT crash landed!"

Somewhere, someone very important had decided that this incident was just too serious to share with the public. I guessed that the "someone" was based in the Pentagon. The military went into full-speed reverse. "The Great Coverup" started.

First Mac Brazel, the rancher who found the wreckage, was silenced. Friends saw him around the town but he was always being escorted by soldiers. He pretended not to see those friends. And he told the radio station a new story.

I had to smile in admiration when I read the new story. If John Smith had been the agent on the scene then he was probably the man responsible for it. The new story was that Brazel had found the wreckage in mid *June*... three or four weeks before he reported it! He supposedly thought it was just something from the air base at

Roswell. At the end of June the reports of flying saucers filled the newspapers. Large rewards were offered for the discovery of an authentic UFO. He remembered the wreckage in his fields, pretended it was a flying saucer and claimed the $3,000 reward.

That was clever. The whole incident was made to appear the product of Mac Brazel's greed. People would be willing to believe that. They *always* like to believe the worst in human nature. When "The Great Coverup" started Brazel was taken into custody by the military. A week later he was free to go. But now he had acquired a brand-new pickup truck.

That was a typical FBI tactic. Make the guy a little afraid then offer him a get-out. I could almost imagine their words: "Retract your story, Brazel, and we'll not only let you go but we'll also make sure you're properly compensated. You wanted that $3,000 reward? I think we could manage that...provided you never reveal the truth."

Brazel walked free, probably believing he'd made a good deal with the authorities. The truth is he had no real choice. He could have refused the $3,000 and easily made a deal with the newspapers for ten times that amount. But if he'd done that, he might just have had some kind of tragic accident. No one in my department at the FBI ever admitted we killed people to keep them quiet. But I guess we all knew we would if it came to it.

My hunch was confirmed when I turned to the file on Sheriff Wilcox's granddaughter. Years after he died she had talked to researchers about her grandfather's part in the Roswell Incident. I took the notes and read them:

My grandfather was a loyal citizen of the United States and he refused to talk about what he saw at Roswell. They made him swear and he kept his oath till the day he died. But my grandmother told me that the Military Police came to the jail and

threatened him. They said that if he ever talked then not only would he be killed...the entire family would be killed.

I'd joined the Bureau to defend the citizens of the United States, but it seemed the job sometimes involved threatening them. But then, witnesses often lie—my police training had taught me that.

I opened a report from an operator at Roswell Radio Station KSWS, a woman named Lydia Sleppy. It seems a call came in from one of the station's reporters. He said he had a great story.

I read what Lydia had to say:

I started taking down details on my teletype machine. I got enough into the UFO crash story to know it was very important. Suddenly the bell rang to signal another call coming in. It appeared on the teletype machine and I read the words: "This is the Federal Bureau of Investigation. You will cease transmitting." The reporter was cut off. The story was killed.

The next file contained a statement from a KSWS reporter named Frank Joyce. It seemed he'd spoken to Brazel, then got that "alien ship" press release. He was about to broadcast it when he too got a call. I read his statement:

The caller identified himself as an officer at the Pentagon. This man said some bad things would happen to me. He was really nasty. I said, "You're talking about the press release from Roswell Air Base?" Bang! The phone went dead. He was gone. That evening I got a call from Mac Brazel. He sounded strained. He told me we hadn't got the story right. I had the feeling he was under tremendous pressure. He said, "Our lives will never be the same again."

So a member of the public had been arrested, a police sheriff threatened, and the local radio station silenced. But what about the military personnel themselves? Surely some of them must have talked about the crash. What did Major Jesse Marcel say about it, I wondered. I found reports about a press conference held by the government, denying any alien findings. A typically smooth FBI coverup. They used the man who'd found the wreckage to present the new story. The FBI used Major Jesse Marcel to tell the public officially what he'd found.

Marcel showed the press what was clearly the remains of a weather balloon. A large foil balloon. He was photographed holding up the shredded pieces. It was all a big mistake, he explained. No flying saucer, just a weather observation balloon. The magic foil was nowhere to be seen.

These weather balloons were launched from Roswell every day. Everyone in the area knew what they looked like. I was pretty sure Marcel would never have mistaken it for an alien craft—even Brazel and Sheriff Wilcox would have recognized the material. The army would never have wasted time sending dozens of men out into the hills to collect a weather balloon. It was obvious what had really happened. They'd found something strange—something extraterrestrial. They announced they'd discovered an alien craft. Then, when they realized just how alien it was, they suddenly decided to change the story. The media quickly invented the weather balloon nonsense to provide an explanation.

I wondered what John Smith had found that convinced him the public had to be protected from it.

The lights of New York City were strung out like bright beads below us as we circled over the airport. The flight had taken only a few hours, but it was another hour before we were finally given permission to land.

For me it seemed like an eternity. I was desperate to meet Agent Smith and solve some of the riddles of Roswell.

CHAPTER FOUR

The FBI is an interstate organization of course, but that doesn't mean its agents are familiar with every corner of the country. I'd been in the Los Angeles Police Department for a couple of years before I transferred to the FBI, and my new chiefs used my local knowledge to work the West Coast.

In my first year I'd been involved in drug trafficking, illegal gambling, and organized crime, but always on a low level. I'd done surveillance and suspect trailing on occasions, but more often I'd used my computer skills to compile statistics and check records for the senior agents in the field. So this was a rare trip to New York for me. I'd never been to the darker, meaner streets of Manhattan.

I'd seen this side of New York City in the movies and I half expected to find a mugger on every dimly lit corner. When the cab I'd hired at the airport stopped in a particularly rundown part of the Lower East side, I remembered Humphrey Bogart's advice in the movie *Casablanca.* He warned a Nazi general not to invade the United States because there were some parts of New York City where it wouldn't be safe for his storm-troopers!

Number 1313, Avenue B was not the coziest of places. It was a brick, four-story building that must once have been red, but was now blackened by years of New York rain. The wooden window frames and door were stained a murky mud color. A rainbow of graffiti was sprayed around the doorway—warning me not to go in. This place had seen better times.

Inside wasn't much of an improvement. The stairs were dark and dusty, and the paintwork was cracked and peeling.

I found apartment 12F on the fourth floor. I quickly ran through the questions in my head. I loosened my tie so I'd look a little less formal and threatening to the old guy— then I tightened it again because I figured that's what he'd expect from a federal agent. I rapped on the door. There was no reply. I tried the handle, but the door was locked.

Even though I had thought of nothing else but Smith during my flight here, I never imagined my subject would be away from his den.

I tramped despondently down the stairs again. In the winter light I could see the silhouette of a white-haired man standing in the doorway. He had a mustache that a walrus would have been proud of. It was snow white, except for a brown stain on one side where a cigarette hung limply from his lip.

"Help you?" he asked. His eyes were suspicious.

"I was looking for John Smith in number 12F," I said.

"You a Mormon? A Jehovah's Witness?" he asked.

"Do I look like a Mormon?" I blinked.

"Nope," he said.

"Then I'm a Jehovah's Witness," I told him. "Any idea where John Smith is?"

"Same place as always at this time," he told me.

I waited. He sucked on his cigarette and coughed. Finally I asked, "Where's that?"

"Diner on the corner," he said.

"How will I recognize him?" I asked.

"Tall. Very tall. And thinner than Arizona rain," he said then turned and went back into the room by the entrance door.

I set off for the corner diner and found Smith without any trouble. He was reading a newspaper as he sat at a table with the cold remains of a black coffee. I stepped forward. "Mr. Smith?" I asked.

He looked up sharply. His face was weathered. It looked even older than his house, but the eyes were still clear. They had the same suspicion in them as Walrus-mustache had. I approached the table and sat down. "My name is Rod Morgan. I'm an agent with the FBI. I'm not on an official assignment, but I am looking into an incident that was reported at Roswell in 1947."

I couldn't be sure, but I might have detected the faintest suggestion of a grin. Otherwise he was giving nothing away. I went on, "I believe you were there?"

He folded his newspaper and leaned forward. "You are not the first to believe that. You were misinformed." His voice was soft but tired.

"The Chief said you wouldn't talk to the media but you *would* talk to an FBI agent," I offered. I took out the letter my chief had printed out in his office and placed it on the table in front of him. He stared at it for a few moments then slipped a hand inside his jacket and pulled out a pair of half-moon glasses. He opened the envelope carefully, slid the paper out and read it two or three times. I knew that what he was really doing was stalling for time while he thought about its contents.

Eventually he looked up at me. His expression was now one of weary humor. "Tell your chief that I've left the FBI. Retired."

"No one leaves the FBI, my chief says," I said with a grin on my face.

He raised one eyebrow and looked at me, then rose stiffly to his feet, turned and walked out of the diner. As Smith crossed the street toward his building I caught up with him. There was no way I was going to give up now.

"The Chief figures I could learn a lot from you," I persisted.

He walked on in silence. I noticed he had a slight limp as he climbed the chipped steps that led up to the doorway of his apartment building. He seemed to be ignoring me, but when we reached the top he turned and stared at me with his sharp but faded eyes.

"I was a lot like you when I was your age," he said. "I'm too old now to play secret agents. Please just leave me alone."

"You're not too old to talk to me, to give me a few hours of your time," I pleaded.

He stood in the half-open door pondering my words. Then with a quick nod of his head he relented.

"Okay kid. I'll talk to you. If your chief thinks its necessary, I better follow the Bureau's orders. Some of the stuff has been unclassified for a few years now anyway. Give me a day to get my notes dusted down and jump-start a few memory cells. Come back tomorrow and maybe I'll have something to tell you."

"Thank you sir," I said.

He took another step inside the door, then stopped and turned back. "Might do me some good to talk. It was kind of sad, son."

"The crash?" I asked and wondered what was so sad about a field of metal shreds.

"No, son," he said softly. "The bodies. Those dead bodies."

Then he was gone.

CHAPTER FIVE

When I arrived back at the building the next morning old Walrus-mustache was lurking just inside the doorway. "Good morning!" I said brightly. "Can I introduce you to the love of Jesus?"

"Can I introduce you to the toe cap of my boot?" he replied sourly.

"I shall pray for you," I said as he disappeared behind his door. "I shall pray that you get flattened by an eighteen-wheel truck."

John Smith was waiting for me. The apartment was modest to say the least, but he made some coffee and we settled down to talk. Outside it was a bitterly cold day. The hot coffee was warming and welcoming.

I had my questions ready. The first thing I wanted to ask him about was the bodies he'd mentioned. But my years of police training had taught me that people talk better when they're relaxed. I thought my best chance of getting any answers was to work up to it slowly. And besides, I was interested in the old guy himself. It was genuine interest, not just police technique. I think he could recognize that too. It seemed to please him, and he opened up to me a little more. He also seemed to guess that I was wondering how he'd ended up living as he did. An agent of his standing should have been living comfortably off a fat government pension.

"I really appreciate this, sir." I said.

He straightened his back and looked wistfully through the window at the colorless sky. "I gave the government over 40 years of service. I risked my life and I sacrificed my health. Vietnam, Korea, China...you see some pretty unhealthy places when you work in counter intelligence. You don't get to stay at the Hilton Hotel. When I was too old and sick to work they gave me a pension... very generously, too. I could have lived comfortably for the rest of my life. But I had a choice between the security of a steady income from a safe pension plan and a possible small fortune on some stock investments. I went for the investments. I was doing well enough until the stock market crashed on Black Monday back in '87. I lost everything. Everything. Now, I have to live like this. It's as bad as it looks. I own the building. But that's about all I own. So take my advice son, when the time comes just take the pension and keep your head down."

"I'll remember your advice," I mumbled.

"Now down to business. You know there are some people who would pay me a tidy sum to tell them what I'm about to tell you. But I take my oath of loyalty seriously."

At last the moment had arrived. He seemed willing to talk about the UFO crash. "You mean, Roswell, Mr. Smith? You were the counter-intelligence agent who went out to examine the wreckage with Major Jesse Marcel?"

He blew a stream of air through his lips in a silent whistle. "Yes. I was. Although I've spent 50 years denying that to just about everyone."

"And what did you make of the stuff you found?" I asked.

"Alien. Beyond a doubt. You just had to touch it. I've encountered nothing like it before or since. The foil stuff sprang back to its original shape and the sheet metal was unbreakable. Did you know, when the army had finished picking up the pieces they didn't find a single rivet, nut, bolt or screw, or welded seam. How was it all held together? Can you tell me that?"

"Possibly some kind of force field. When the force field generator failed, then the shell fell apart," I said. I'd read a fair amount about the crash on the Internet. But the information there was all speculation. No one had access to a firsthand witness the way I had now. "Do you remember seeing any kind of power source? Generator? Turbine? Electrical coils?"

"Ah, no," Agent Smith said. "That'd be with the *main* part of the crew cabin. It would be where the bodies were found."

I got a crazy creepy feeling at the back of my neck. It's a feeling I always get when something is about to turn seriously weird.

"What bodies were they, Mr. Smith?"

He looked surprised. "I thought you'd read up about the Roswell Incident."

"Yes, sir," I said quietly. "A crashed flying saucer that was recovered by the air force who told a story about a weather balloon."

"Ah, then you haven't linked it to the other incident. The crash at Corona?"

"No, sir. What happened at Corona?"

"They found the bodies at Corona," he said. I was beginning to wonder if this was for real.

CHAPTER SIX

The old man explained. He spoke slowly but with a soothing rhythm like a mother reading a bedtime story.

"I was a young counter-intelligence agent assigned to White Sands Missile Range about a hundred miles from Roswell. The stuff they were doing there was top secret, you understand? They were working with German rocket scientists, World War II experts, to develop a U.S. missile defense system. The trouble was the Russians also had German expertise, and we knew they were developing something similar."

"There was a race on," I nodded. "When World War II ended the Cold War began."

"That's right," he said. "The Russians would have given anything to get their hands on the White Sands secrets. I was one of the counter-intelligence agents assigned to stop them."

"That was a big responsibility," I said.

He blew out his thin cheeks. "You have to remember I was just one member of a big team. And a very junior member, too. They didn't put me in charge of the operation!"

I grinned. "I know what you mean. I get most of the standard jobs myself. Once I had to watch an empty house for a week in case a suspect returned to it. But he'd been arrested and locked away for two days before my superiors remembered I was even there and took me off surveillance!"

The old man chuckled. "There's a lot of that in the FBI. Long hours of routine work. And the more routine the work then the more junior the officer assigned to it. But it has to be done."

I nodded. Secret-agent movies never show how dull intelligence work can sometimes be!

"Don't forget that in the 1940s we were sending rockets up into the atmosphere for the first time," he explained. "The results weren't always predictable. Sometimes they crashed and we had to arrange a quick coverup. One or two of those rockets had experimental nuclear warheads. We were on constant alert to get an agent to the crash sites before anyone else. Of course some of the missiles were spotted in flight by the public, and we had to think of some other cover story. But in the summer of '47 it all went a little crazy."

"The UFO scare?" I asked.

"The UFO scare. A pilot saw one of our experimental rockets and reported it. The story was all over the national press and radio before we could stop it. Soon everyone was seeing lights in the sky. A lot of those people were lying, of course, and some just might have seen our own rockets...but there were a few reports that *no one* could explain." Smith replied. "It seemed as if there was something really happening up there that we didn't know about."

"Alien craft? That's a bit of a coincidence, isn't it? It seems a bit too uncanny that they arrived just as we were sending up our own UFOs." I said.

He screwed up his face, rose stiffly to his feet and walked to the window. "That's one way of looking at it. But there is another explanation. Let's just suppose that these aliens had been watching Earth for a long time—I don't mean a few years...I mean *thousands* of years. They watched us crawling out of caves, then building pyramids, then spluttering up into the air in wood and string airplanes. Finally they observed us as we invented rocket propulsion. What would these aliens do then?"

I shrugged. "Take a closer look?"

He turned and looked at me. "That's right. Take a closer look. Start to send their spacecraft over the United States to take a look at White Sands...maybe even track the missiles and examine them when they landed. There were several reports coming in from pilots claiming to have been tracked by strange craft."

"And then one of the aliens' spacecraft crashed?" I asked incredulously.

"We didn't know that at first," Agent Smith said slowly. "But among the dozens of reports we thought there might be one or two worth a closer look. There just weren't enough agents to investigate every sighting. As it happened, the Roswell report was just one of twenty that day. My senior officer thought it might be worth a look. After all, it wasn't so very far from White Sands, and it could well have been one of our experimental rockets. Even though I was a pretty junior agent I was sent out to take a look."

"And you found the wreckage?"

"Yes. I went out to the Roswell crash site and took a look at what the rancher Mac Brazel had found. I knew at once it was different from anything I'd ever seen before. It certainly wasn't one of our missiles. I quickly realized that if news had leaked out about an alien crash then the whole world would have been down there, disturbing things. Then that fool public information officer Haut released a press bulletin that said they'd found a flying saucer. When the Pentagon found out, they told me to kill the story—invent some new explanation and get the witnesses to withdraw their original statements immediately. I guess we could have got out of that one easily enough."

"But something must have happened to make the Pentagon take it so seriously. They've been covering this up for 50 years! There must be more to it than a few fragments of metal. Right?"

He chewed on the corner of his lip and nodded his head. "There is more to the story than that. And I was the man at the center of it all. There was something so fantastic that even today the government don't want to admit it ever happened."

"The bodies?" I prompted.

"The bodies," he agreed.

CHAPTER SEVEN

The old man took a faded diary out from a suitcase under his bed. It was bound in worn black leather and the pages had yellowed around the edges. He read silently for five minutes then turned back to me. "We'd been sending up reconnaissance planes to check for any other wreckage, and one crew came in with a fresh report. They said that a capsule had been spotted about two to three miles from the Roswell site. Nearer to a place called Corona. It looked as if it could have been part of the same craft."

"You think the alien crew had ejected from the main craft before it disintegrated at Roswell?" I asked.

John Smith nodded slowly. "That's the way it looked. The difference was that this time there were bodies lying beside the capsule."

"Aliens?" I asked. I could feel the hairs on the back of my neck starting to stick up again.

"The observation plane crew couldn't tell what they were from that height," the old man answered. "All we knew was that there was something very strange going on. There were lots of possibilities. One of the things we considered was that the thing was a Russian experimental craft—that was one of the reasons I had been sent down to investigate. Another possibility was that it was a U.S. craft—other secret bases like White Sands were experimenting with space flight and new types of aircraft that we knew nothing about. Or it could have been aliens linked to those UFO reports that'd been going around for a couple of weeks. Anyway, whatever it was there were bodies to be seen—maybe even survivors. And I had to be the first to get to them. The Pentagon didn't want the public to stumble upon them first, and I was the agent closest to the scene. I just had to keep people out of the area."

"By sealing it off?" I asked.

Agent Smith sucked the air through his teeth. "No way I could do that, not even with the cooperation of the military. The area was huge and deserted. There aren't enough soldiers in the country to throw a ring of guards in a circle around both sites. No. The only way to keep people away was by making them lose interest in the whole affair. So I came up with the weather balloon story."

I nodded, beginning to understand. "I wondered why there was the sudden change of story."

"Unfortunately I was a little late getting there. There were no real roads in the Corona crash area—just dirt tracks, so it took me a while. Then, when I got there I found some people had already beaten me to it. There was a group of archeologists working in the area. They'd caught a glimpse of the capsule and gone up to investigate. When they'd arrived, they'd seen the same thing that the spotter plane had caught sight of. A broken-up capsule with four humanoid bodies lying beside it. We'll never know if the crash killed them or if they staggered out of the wreckage and died in our atmosphere...the way you'd die if you stepped out on the Moon."

"So what were the aliens like, Mr. Smith?" I asked.

"Small. Around four feet tall, I guess. They were wearing gray one-piece suits and looked quite human in some ways—two skinny arms and two skinny legs—but their heads were weird...pear-shaped and way too large for their bodies. Their skin was leathery and they all had huge eyes—black and glassy. Tiny mouths too."

"What did you do with the witnesses? Kill them?" I demanded.

The old man's eyes narrowed. "We were experts in cover stories...or you may prefer to call it lying...but we'd never have killed unless we absolutely had to. Dead citizens take a lot of explaining, and anyway, son, we were sworn to protect the lives of U.S. citizens...not exterminate them. No. These archeologists were men and women of science. They understood the importance of keeping this sort of thing secret till we understood it better. We persuaded them to falsify their diaries so they could never be traced to that part of New Mexico on that particular date. And we asked them to keep quiet."

"And if they hadn't?" I persisted.

Agent Smith drained his coffee and pulled a face at the bitter taste. "We were pretty confident that they understood the seriousness of the situation. But Mac Brazel was a rancher. Not as bright as the archeologists. He was keen to talk. First we held him in custody for a week—he didn't like that. Then we threatened him just a little so that afterward, when we offered him the money, he was glad enough to take it."

"And the archeologists have kept quiet all this time?"

"No. They did at first, but some have begun to talk in the last few years. The case is beginning to attract interest again. I think maybe the Pentagon is planning a new cover story...I'm just not sure what it is."

I stood up and stretched. "And are the witnesses safe, Agent Smith? Surely after 50 years, no one's going to get hurt if they talk?"

"They're safe enough, I guess."

I walked to the window and looked down into the gray-black street. "Have you ever had to kill someone in the line of duty, Mr. Smith?" I asked.

"Of course," he said and his voice was flat and bleak. "Don't think they don't come back and haunt me some nights."

"Innocent people, Mr. Smith? People like those archeologists who were just unlucky enough to be in the wrong place at the wrong time?"

His face was as expressionless as a mask. "Sometimes the good of the nation is more important than the good of one individual," he said.

"Do you ever worry that you know too much?"

He nodded. "Yes," he sighed. "But that's part of the job." He looked at me without emotion.

"Is it something you get used to?" I pressed. If I was going to give my allegiance to the FBI, I just had to know what the consequences were.

"It becomes part of you. You learn to handle it. And just for the record, you can report back to your chief that my lips are still sealed."

"I sure will, sir," I assured him. I hoped I would be able to keep secrets like that.

I returned to the problems of Roswell, Corona, and the coverup. "What I'd really like to know is what happened to all this evidence? The wreckage? The bodies?"

"They were all taken off to Wright-Patterson Air Base in Dayton, Ohio, to be examined," he said. "I organized the removal myself. And that's when I made two serious mistakes." He held up a hand and counted on his thin, pale fingers. "One: I let a civilian witness see the bodies. And two: I thought I was dealing with four corpses...but I wasn't!"

CHAPTER EIGHT

"They were alive!" I croaked in amazement.

"*One* was still alive," the old man breathed. "At least, that's what they said later. Remember this was three days after the crash so he—or she or it—was in a bad way. Deeply unconscious. It wasn't till they got back to the hospital at Wright-Patterson Air Base that someone saw it move. Now I didn't see it myself. I was too busy trying to cover up the discovery of the capsule. My job was simply to get the bodies to the hospital for examination. There was no way I wanted to stay around and see them cutting up little gray men! Anyway I was too busy creating a new problem for the Pentagon," Smith said ruefully.

I was hooked by the old guy's story and I wanted to hear the end. "What was that you said about the civilian witness?" I asked.

He went to his desk drawer and pulled out some magazines. *UFO Monthly* was on the top. "Mortician's Roswell Revelations" the cover said in bright red lettering against a black-and-white photograph of a pear-shaped face with shining black alien eyes.

He handed the magazine to me. I opened it and eagerly began to read. It was about a man named Glenn Dennis. Dennis was the mortician in Roswell in 1947. Around the time of the Roswell crash he began to get calls from the air base asking for the smallest coffins Dennis had— about four feet long. They also had to be capable of being sealed. And they began to ask him questions about chemical preserving liquids. Dennis was puzzled. I read his reported statement:

I talked to them four or five times in the

afternoon. They would keep calling back and asking me different questions about the bodies they said they had. What they really wanted to know was how they could move those bodies. I said, "Look, what do these bodies look like?" and they said, "I don't know, but I'll tell you one thing; this happened some time ago." They mentioned that they'd been exposed to the elements for several days.

I tried to put myself in Agent Smith's shoes. A civilian witness was the last thing the Pentagon wanted. If Dennis saw anything positive then he'd surely have to be dealt with. I needed to know how much the mortician had witnessed. "But Glenn Dennis didn't see the aliens, did he?"

"No!" the old man said. "He almost did, though. Seems Dennis's hearse doubled as an ambulance, and that night he took an injured soldier to the air base hospital where they were examining the aliens. He helped the soldier into the hospital, in the hope of seeing a certain nurse he was friendly with. Here's his statement." He leaned across and pointed to a paragraph lower down the same page of the magazine:

There were two Military Police at the door and I started to get out of the ambulance and go into the hospital. I wouldn't have gotten as far as I did if I hadn't parked in the emergency area. The doors were open to the military ambulances. The wreckage was in there and there was a Military Policeman on each side. I saw all the wreckage.

I don't know what it was but I knew there was something going on. There were a lot of very high-ranking officers there. They were really shaken up.

I saw the nurse coming toward me. She looked surprised to see me. She said, "How did you get in here? My God, you are going to get killed."

I was going to the Coke machine to get us a Coke when this big red-headed colonel said, "What's he doing here?"

He hollered at the MPs and that's when all hell broke loose. These two MPs grabbed me by the arms, lifted me right off my feet and carried me clear outside. I didn't walk, they carried me. And they told me to get the heck out of there.

It didn't stop there. They followed me back to the funeral parlor and told me, "If you open your mouth you'll be put so far back in jail they'll have to feed you with peas through a peashooter."

I just laughed and said, "Get lost!"

I sighed. "So Dennis wasn't really a problem for you. He wasn't like a firsthand witness...someone who actually saw the bodies in the hospital."

John Smith took the magazine and turned the page. "I think you'll find that the nurse friend of Dennis told him what she'd seen."

Dennis's statement went on:

She said, "There were three bodies. They looked kind of like ancient Chinese. They were small and frail and had no hair. Their noses didn't protrude and their eyes were pretty deep and their ears were just indentations. They didn't have thumbs...just four fingers like tentacles with suction caps on the end. Two of them were mangled beyond everything, but there was one of them that was in pretty good condition." The nurse drew a picture of the creatures for me, but burned it afterward because she was scared of what they'd do to her if they found it.

"I thought there were four bodies," I said frowning.

"Three dead and one alive," John Smith said carefully. "At least that's one of the rumors that went around. The nurse just saw the dead ones they were examining. But when they were unpacking the bodies, someone noticed movement in the fourth alien. It seems they put it in some kind of intensive care unit. It died later. I always wonder if I could have saved it, if only I'd spotted some sign of life when I found the bodies."

We both fell silent at the thought. The first chance of human contact with another race from the stars.

CHAPTER NINE

John continued to tell me other pieces of assorted information.

"It's quite a story," I said finally. "But there are a lot of secondhand reports. There's no statement from the nurse herself—only a statement from Dennis who reported what she said. Not the kind of evidence that would ever be allowed in court."

"Yes. But the pilot of the plane that took the bodies to the air base, Captain Oliver Henderson—he saw the bodies as well," John Smith frowned. "There were just too many people around for a single agent to cope with."

"But Henderson never actually went public with his sighting." I said. It was the first time I had contradicted him. "In the magazine report you just showed me, it's his friend talking...he says Henderson told him about looking at the bodies in a crate. Anyway, Henderson's dead now." I looked up. "There's only one living person who actually says he saw the bodies. That's you, Mr. Smith."

The old man leaned back on his creaking chair. "I know, son. I know. I'm probably the last living person to have seen, firsthand, those aliens. Remember, I was a young agent at the time—the surgeons, the air-search crews, and even the archeologists were all older people. They're dead now. But you were asking about the wreckage."

"Isn't that evidence?" I said.

"Well, you should know that there's a strange story about the documents relating to that wreckage," he smiled grimly. "In 1984, a bunch of classified files known as the Majestic 12 documents found their way into the possession of a movie director. The Majestic 12 documents were supposed to have been reports written to the President in the early fifties. But they didn't come to light until the eighties—that's when there was a new interest in Roswell and Corona. The reports point to strange happenings at Wright-Patterson Air Base."

"So, the reports say the wreckage was at Wright-Patterson," I said slowly. "Well the FBI has almost certainly moved the stuff since those reports were published."

John Smith leaned forward in his creaking chair and said quietly, "You still don't quite understand the way the FBI thinks, do you?"

I guess I blushed a little. "I haven't been with them very long," I admitted.

He nodded. "I was with them for over 40 years. I was retired when the Majestic 12 documents were published. But I have a nose for FBI tricks and I knew right away what had happened. The Majestic 12 documents were released by the FBI *themselves!*"

"Because they wanted the public to know where the wreckage was?" I blinked. I was being stupid and still didn't see what he was getting at.

"No," he said gently, like a teacher to a slow-witted pupil. "The Majestic 12 documents were almost certainly forged. Probably released by the government to make the whole Roswell scare look like a fake. Do you understand? If the wreckage hasn't been buried in the Earth's deepest hole then it may be in the locked vaults of the Pentagon. It may be on the mantel of the Oval Office in the White House...it may be anywhere in the world, except one place. It will most certainly *not* be at Wright-Patterson Air Base."

I nodded and cursed my own stupidity. "The documents were released to put researchers off the scent. We have a word for that tactic."

John Smith sat up straight and gave me a withering look. "Agent Morgan, I am not *that* old. We had the same word for it when I was an active agent."

I winced. "Sorry, Mr. Smith."

"And the word is disinformation!"

I nodded. "And if they are still putting out disinformation 40 years after the event they must still think the truth about Roswell is too dangerous to release."

"Too dangerous, or too embarrassing. Who knows?"

His creased face split into a grin. "Well, that's about it kid."

But we continued to talk for several hours more as the wintry sky darkened outside and the room grew colder. I learned a lot from him. He helped me to understand the kind of life I was likely to have as an agent.

"Be sure it's what you want," he said. And I knew I'd never forget one of the last things we talked about.

"When you're young you never worry about death because it seems so far away. But you get afraid of death when you're middle-aged. Then you discover that there's something far worse than death and you're not afraid of it anymore."

"What's worse than death?" I had asked him.

"Old age, son. Old age." Something about the way he'd called me "son" this time made me shiver. He smiled. "You see your friends grow old...then you see them lose their dignity. That's the hard part. Losing your dignity." He threw his head back and laughed. "You know what they say. First you start by forgetting to pull your zipper up... then you end by forgetting to pull it down."

I laughed. I had no idea then that he was so close to death.

We also talked about his fears of being spied on, and he told me whom he suspected. Eventually it became so dark that his face looked like a pale mask against a black velvet background.

I left John Smith's apartment with that solemn image of him engraved in my mind. I had been shocked by the strain the Roswell secrets had caused him. And as I walked toward the brighter side of town, I resolved to keep in contact with the old agent—he had taught me a lot.

I didn't realize then that I would never have the chance to talk to him again.

Chapter Ten

When I returned to Los Angeles I hurried back to my office even though I was due an extra two days' leave. I was impatient to see the boss, tell him my decision and finally be accepted into the FBI as a full-fledged agent.

I punched his office number into the phone and heard his secretary answer. I heard her hesitate when I told her my name. "He's on leave."

My heart sank. "Till when?" I asked miserably.

There was another long pause. "Indefinitely," she said.

I shook my head. "Indefinitely?"

"Early retirement," she said.

"But my probation...who do I see about my promotion to full agent status?" I asked.

She paused and I heard muttering as she put a hand over the phone and talked to someone. At last she said, "Mr. Ellis, your new senior officer, will see you."

"Can I make an appointment, then," I asked wearily.

"No, he'll see you now," she said abruptly, and the phone went dead.

I straightened my tie. I wished I could have straightened my brain as easily. I was in a daze as I walked along the corridor, took an elevator to the seventh floor and stepped out. I tapped on the glass panel of the Chief's door. "Come in," a voice answered.

There were two men behind the desk, but I didn't recognize either of them. One was seated and one was standing. The one standing looked tough. He never said a word the whole time I was in the office, and his eyes never left me.

The seated man had one of those plastic-smooth faces that

could have been any age from 30 to 50. His icy cold eyes watched me intently. "My name is Ellis and I am your new case officer," he said. His voice was as smooth as his face.

"My last boss..."

"Made one mistake too many," he cut in. "He has volunteered to retire,"

"What mistake?" I asked, bewildered.

"He should never have sent you to see John Smith," Ellis explained.

"I learned a lot from Agent Smith," I argued. "He had integrity. He has witnessed one of the most amazing stories in the world and he's told no one for 50 years."

Ellis snorted. "He told *you*," he said shortly.

"Yes, but..." I stammered.

"You have to realize, Agent Smith was ill."

"He had a weak heart, I know," I replied.

"No...ill in the head," the man told me. He tapped his forehead. "He had delusions. He believed that he'd seen aliens and a flying saucer. These ramblings were harmless, but you must understand they were the imaginings of a senile old man."

"But something *did* happen at Roswell and Corona," I insisted. "Something so secret that we've classified the information for 50 years!"

"It's no secret any longer," he shrugged. "I guess I can tell you the truth. But I'm afraid it's not the story you'll have heard from Agent Smith." He looked up at me and his face was without emotion. The lies came easily to him. I almost believed him. "The truth is the Germans had rocket missiles called V-2s that they used against London at the end of World War II," he said. "After the war, we brought a lot of German rocket scientists over here to make similar missiles for us. The idea was to build them before the Communists did. One of the things we wanted to do was find the effect of high-altitude flight on the human body. We were hoping to send manned rockets up into the atmosphere. But before we tested it on men, we tested it on monkeys." His voice was smooth. Persuasive.

"And the test rocket crashed?" I asked flatly.

"You've seen old video footage of the Apollo Space Program? We had parachute splashdowns in the ocean for those flights. For the Monkey Missile project we thought we might be able to land them back on the test range. That July 2, 1947 rocket didn't make it. It fell 75 miles short of the White Sands range. The parachute was a new type of foil we were developing. It disintegrated into shreds with the forces. That's what they found at Roswell."

"There were aliens on board," I said. "There were witnesses!"

He almost smiled again. "Not aliens. Monkeys."

I stared at him blankly.

"Monkeys. They were hairless because the heat of re-entry singed off their fur. The depressurization made their eyes pop out. What else do you think looks like a small human with skinny arms and legs? Monkeys."

"Were they taken back to the Wright-Patterson for examination?" I questioned him.

"Of course they were. That was the whole point of the experiment. They were examined to discover the effects of high-altitude flight on their bodies. Hey, you came back here on a plane, didn't you, son?"

"Yes."

"So the cabin was pressurized. Our scientists learned to do that after the Monkey Rocket type of experiment. Punch a hole in the side of your airliner when it's really high and your eyes would pop out too."

I wanted to be out of the room. Away from this man who was tearing John Smith's story to shreds. I couldn't bear to hear him being discredited like this. I said, "The foil parachute—the one that shredded and failed—I suppose that's what Mac Brazel found at Roswell?"

He nodded.

"And you made up a cover story about a weather balloon because you didn't want the Russians finding out about your rocket program?"

"You're a smart guy," he said, and I could see him relax. "Forget the stories about aliens and little green men..."

"Gray," I said. "They were gray."

"Whatever," he snapped impatiently. "We'll soon have an answer for the crazies like ex-Agent Smith who believe in little gray men. You'll see. Watch your TV for a show on Roswell. You wait and see. You're on probation aren't you?" he asked me.

I nodded. "Yes, sir."

He rose to his feet, leaned forward and said softly, "Then I'll give you a piece of advice: The official line is that Roswell and Corona never happened. Do I make myself clear?"

"Any clearer and you'd be invisible," I said.

"I'm glad we understand one another," Ellis smiled.

I understood. I understood that even after 50 years no one was prepared to talk about Roswell. The FBI wanted to squash the story. They even seemed to be calling one of their former agents a liar.

I was no longer sure I wanted to join this club. I couldn't help myself. I believed in John Smith and I told them so.

Ellis looked over his shoulder at the heavyweight observer behind him. The man gave a tiny shake of the head.

Then my new boss sat down again and began to write on some kind of form. He scribbled quickly and didn't look up. "Your year as an agent has been interesting, but your character profile indicates that you would be more use to your country back in the police force," he said coldly.

"You could be right," I replied.

I turned on my heel and left the office. I walked quickly down the corridor, past the dragon on guard outside the classified fileroom.

A room I'd never have a key to. Secrets I'd never get to read now. But I had Agent John Smith's story. I could have chosen to believe that his words were those of a rambling old man. But I didn't.

I chose to believe him.

Sometime in December I tried to contact John Smith again. I wanted to know if he'd care to take a break in California. It would be warmer than New York for Christmas. I'd have paid his air fare and given him a bed in my apartment. To be honest, I also wanted to hear him talk some more about Roswell and Corona. Especially Corona and those aliens.

I called his apartment. A voice I didn't recognize answered the phone. I asked for John.

"You a relative?" the unfamiliar voice asked.

"No, a friend."

"Didn't know he had friends."

"Can I speak to him?"

"Only if you have the phone number to heaven...or hell," sniffed the voice unkindly. "John Smith died last Tuesday. I'm a friend of the family's. Sorting out some of his papers."

"How?" I whispered. I didn't trust my voice. I felt choked.

"Pneumonia. They figure he'd been dead a day or more when they found him."

I put the phone down and sat motionless for an hour, trying to make sense of it all. At last I found the nerve to call back and ask about the funeral arrangements. It seemed I wouldn't make the funeral, but there was still one last thing I could do for the old man.

The last witness of Roswell had one final trip to make.

CHAPTER ELEVEN

When the spring came I went out to New Mexico.

Like any good investigator I had to go and look at the scene of the incident. The desert is very striking in the spring. The arid expanse of baked earth that surrounded me for miles in every direction had a certain majesty all of its own.

But there was no alien metal scattered there. Researchers had returned time and again, but found nothing. John Smith's cleanup operation had been too thorough.

I'd done a lot more research into the investigators who'd studied the Roswell and Corona incidents. I checked the maps of the crash location. I drove down the roads that John Smith and Major Jesse Marcel had driven down 50 years before. Those roads were no better now. I had to hike the two miles to the wreckage site.

I stopped for lunch at the stone outcrop where the bodies had been found. Afterward, I held a large clay pot in my hands and stared up at the clear blue sky, wondering if aliens had ghosts. I looked around me at the wind-polished rocks. Crows were being blown around the sky like black confetti. Very fitting for what I was about to do. "I wanted to believe you, John," I whispered. "No matter what the agent in that room said about you losing your mind. I want to believe that there are gray men out there. I don't want to think we're alone. But to tell you the truth, I just don't know what to think anymore."

I took a deep breath, lifted the lid off the urn and looked at the ashes inside. He'd had the best cremation that money could buy. "Well, John," I said. "I thought you'd like it here. New York City isn't all it's cracked up to be. Especially when you're in no condition to enjoy the nightlife. Er...this is where it started. So it seems right to finish it here."

I tipped the urn forward and the ashes were swept away on the wind before they even touched the ground. The gray curtain faded to nothing. "Dust to dust and ashes to ashes," I called after the vanishing cloud. Then, in a whisper, I said, "Good-bye, John."

The old man's secret drifted away on the wind. Almost...

I slipped a faded black diary into my pocket. This personal record of Roswell had escaped the grasping hands of the FBI. It had escaped being locked away in a secret government file, far from public reach. As I held John's diary in my hand, I tried to make sense of it all. Later as I watched the sunset, my eyes aimlessly roamed the skies—desperately searching for an answer to this mystery.

Would the Roswell Incident ever be cleared up?

As I gazed at the myriad stars above me, a disturbing thought suddenly entered my mind:

Perhaps someone, somewhere up there, was wondering the same thing.

GLOSSARY

BALL LIGHTNING
An incredibly rare kind of lightning that occurs only in freak weather conditions. Unlike forked or sheet lightning, this variety appears in the sky as a slow-moving ball of electrical activity. Ball lightning has been used as an explanation for many UFO sightings.

CIC
(COUNTER INTELLIGENCE CORPS)
Military department working within the U.S. army. It bears no direct relation to the CIA (Central Intelligence Agency), which was just in the process of creation in 1947. When the CIA became fully operational in the late 1940s, the CIC closed down and folded up.

DISINFORMATION
False information released deliberately to mislead people.

EXTRATERRESTRIAL
An object or living being that has come from outside the Earth and its atmosphere.

FBI
(FEDERAL BUREAU OF INVESTIGATION)
Division of the U.S. Justice Department, run from the national headquarters in Washington, D.C. The FBI is the most important investigating division of the government. Part

of the Bureau deals with law enforcement and looks into federal crimes, including kidnapping, espionage, and treason. The FBI also gathers information on people or groups that could threaten national security.

MAJESTIC 12 DOCUMENTS
A series of documents, released in the 1980s. These reports suggest that all analysis of the Roswell and Corona findings took place at Wright-Patterson Air Base. It is possible that these files are fakes, perhaps even generated by the U.S. government itself.

MONKEY MISSILE PROJECT
Allegedly the U.S. government used this project as a test run for the first manned space rockets.

WHITE SANDS MISSILE RANGE
Government missile testing and development site about 100 miles from Roswell. Working with German rocket experts captured at the end of World War II, the U.S. military was secretly using these scientists' skills to develop a missile defense system.

UFO
(UNIDENTIFIED FLYING OBJECT)
An unexplainable light or object that is either seen in the sky or detected on radar.

V-2
Early guided missiles used by the Germans during World War II. The V-2s were driven by rocket power and could fly faster than the speed of sound.

BIOGRAPHIES

This story contains fictional characters investigating a true-life mystery. Before you look at the facts and make up your own mind, here's a brief biography of the characters:

MAC BRAZEL
(ACTUAL CHARACTER)
Rancher who first found the wreckage at Roswell. Although he reported that he'd discovered the remains of an alien spacecraft he later retracted this statement unconditionally. In somewhat mysterious circumstances, Brazel claimed he had only found the shredded foil from a weather balloon.

THE CHIEF
(FICTIONAL)
Rod Morgan's senior officer at the FBI, who instructs him to hear John Smith's story before he decides he is ready to become a full-fledged agent.

GLENN DENNIS
(ACTUAL CHARACTER)
Town mortician who claimed to have been questioned by staff at Wright-Patterson Air Base and who supplied the coffins for the "alien" bodies. Dennis also provided a witness report from a nurse who allegedly examined

the bodies from Corona.

SENIOR OFFICER ELLIS
(FICTIONAL)
Rod's new chief. Discredits John Smith's
testimony and bars Rod from the FBI for not
accepting the official account of the Roswell
Incident.

MAJOR JESSE MARCEL
(ACTUAL CHARACTER)
First of the air force staff on the scene of the
crash. He was aware that the debris was
alien and went along with the announcement
of a flying saucer find. However, he was
forced to change his story and agree with the
cover story of a crashed weather balloon.
After retiring from the air force he finally
admitted his certainty that an alien craft had
landed at Roswell.

ROD MORGAN
(FICTIONAL)
FBI trainee, about to graduate to a full-
fledged agent if he can accept the discipline
needed to keep FBI secrets.

AGENT JOHN SMITH
(ACTUAL CHARACTER, DISGUISED NAME)
The counter-intelligence agent who was the
first government official to come across the
Roswell and Corona crashes. Loosely based on
real-life agent Sheridan Cavitt. He passed
messages between the air base at Roswell and
the FBI in the Pentagon. Junior in rank to

people like Jesse Marcel but with the power of the Pentagon behind him, he could tell the air force what to tell the public about the crash—even if it meant changing the story after just four hours and lying about a weather balloon crash.

SHERIFF GEORGE A. WILCOX (ACTUAL CHARACTER)
Local sheriff whom Mac Brazel first approached with the Roswell wreckage.

CLASSIFIED FILES

Are the Roswell stories true? Is the U.S. government going to great lengths to hide the facts from the American people and the rest of the world? Look at some of the arguments for and against the alien theory:

A Roswell crash NEVER happened because

It would be impossible to keep it secret. Too many people, military and civilian, knew too much. Dozens of soldiers helped to clear up the site, the pieces of the wreckage were transported by air crews, packed by staff, and stored somewhere by other officials. The bodies were examined by medical experts and government observers. Hundreds of people were involved. Someone, somewhere, would have talked during the 30 years after the find.

BUT:

Many people *have* talked. Most of these people are intelligent and responsible—air force officers, archeologists, and an undertaker. Have they all suddenly decided to lie? Besides, evidence shows that it *is* possible to keep secrets for a long time. For example, the Stealth Bomber was already flying before the public were even told it was being developed!

People in the United States have more

right to examine secret documents than they used to have. After 40 years documents are "declassified." This means that they are available for inspection by anyone who asks. So if there had been secret documents about an alien craft crashing at Roswell, they would have come to light by now.

BUT:

In practice, not all files *are* declassified. The military can bend the rules. They can say, "It is not in the interests of national security to declassify these files." Roswell Incident investigators have been allowed to see only ten percent of the air force's files for this period, even though they are nearly 50 years old.

The remains of a flying saucer and its crew could not remain hidden for 50 years. Someone would know where it is stored. Of all the pieces scattered over the crash site, surely some must have survived—perhaps hidden in the rugged terrain or taken home as a souvenir by one of the military searchers?

BUT:

It *is* possible to hide things. The military have nuclear weapons, missiles, and bombs with about 20,000 nuclear warheads. These are well hidden from enemy spies or terrorists. If they can hide so much weaponry, then the military could easily hide the debris from an alien spacecraft and even the bodies of its crew.

The Roswell crash DID happen because

The government is obviously keeping

something secret. If the wreckage was just a weather balloon, then why did the military go to such lengths to lie and cover up the evidence? The rancher Mac Brazel was held for over a week. Would they do that if there was nothing to hide?

The original finders issued a press release openly admitting that a flying saucer had been found. They did this because they wanted good relationships with the people in the local towns, many of whom might have seen or heard something. It was only when the government got to hear about it and decided to classify the information that the coverup started.

Five hundred people interviewed agree that something strange happened at Roswell in 1947. Five hundred people can't all be liars, can they? One man who refuses to talk, FBI Agent Sheridan Cavitt (Agent John Smith), probably knows as much as anyone. If there's no mystery about Roswell then why doesn't he simply say so?

THE 1947 UFO SENSATION

Why didn't the landing of a UFO cause a worldwide sensation back in 1947? If it really happened, then why was it largely ignored for more than 20 years.

One answer might be that the Roswell Incident happened at the height of a "season" of UFO sightings. UFO reports often come in sudden bursts, then everything goes quiet for years. This means that either:

a) UFOs visit our planet at intervals, are seen by many people, then go away for a few years. OR

b) Someone imagines they have seen a UFO and hysteria spreads. Soon everyone imagines they have seen something. After a while people lose interest and find something new to become excited about. OR

c) A mixture of **a)** and **b)**. Someone sees a genuine UFO and reports it. More and more people then imagine they have seen something. The later reports are so confused or silly that no one believes the first, *true* report.

It is possible that something like **c)** happened in June and July 1947. Here are just a few of the hundreds of UFO sightings reported at that time:

Date: June 24, 1947

Reporter: Kenneth Arnold, pilot.

Place: On a search-rescue mission near Mount Rainier, Washington.

Sighting: Nine objects sighted, flying north to south at 9,022 feet and approximately 1,695 miles per hour— faster than any known craft could fly at that time. First modern UFO report.

UFO: Boomerang-shaped craft that skipped along like "saucers skipping across the water."

Date: June 24, 1947

Reporter: Fred Johnson, mining prospector

Place: Cascade mountains, Columbia river area

Sighting: Five to six craft flying overhead. Made his compass spin wildly. First report of the effects of UFOs on instruments.

UFO: Disk-shaped with small tail, 30 feet long. Three feet in diameter, reflecting sunlight from its shiny surface.

Date: June 26, 1947

Reporter: Royce R. Knight, airport manager, and Charles Moore

Place: Cedar City, Utah

Sighting: Single object in flight to east. In view just seconds before disappearing at a high speed. First report of an explosion.

UFO: Moore: Like a bright meteor with no exhaust or flames. Knight: Disintegrated into a ball of blue flame.

Date: June 27, 1947

Reporter: Ms. Cummins and Ms. Dill

Place: Capitan, New Mexico

Sighting: Flying object appeared to land in the nearby hills. First report of a landing.

UFO: Yellow flames came from craft and it emitted a whistling sound.

Date: July 7, 1947

Reporter: Vernon Baird, P38 airplane pilot

Place: 29,855 feet over Tobacco Root Mountains, Montana

Sighting: A formation of disks following his plane. As he watched one fell away and came toward him. The backwash from the P38 tore the UFO apart and it crashed to the forest below. First report of a UFO crash.

UFO: About 15 feet in diameter and shaped like a yo-yo.

Date: July 8, 1947
Reporter: Unnamed merchant seaman
Place: Houston, Texas
Sighting: Saucer landed and four-foot-tall alien with a head the size of a basketball emerged, greeted the seaman then climbed back in and took off. One of the first sightings of small aliens.

UFO: Silver saucer

Date: July 8, 1947
Reporter: Mac Brazel, rancher
Place: Roswell, New Mexico
Sighting: Remains of a flying disk found on ranch. First report of a saucer being found. Report changed six hours later to say the wreckage was in fact from a weather balloon.

UFO: Made from silvery foil.

The reports began to die out by the end of July 1947. The last report (Mac Brazel's) became known, years later, as the Roswell Incident. It's easy to see why it was not sensational news; it was lost among stories of little men with basketball-sized heads and exploding meteors!

It was also competing with UFO stories from all around the world, from Australia to Russia.

Naturally a lot of sensible people scoffed at the stories. There were so many inconsistencies. The UFOs were shaped like a yo-yo—or a boomerang—or a saucer. They were blue, or red, or silver. They were silent, or whistling. They gave off no exhaust, or they gave off yellow flames.

If there were any genuine sightings in the mass of reports then they were disbelieved. It's just possible, of course, that all of the reports were true, and in one month, Earth was visited by thousands of alien craft in hundreds of different shapes and sizes!

But that's one answer to the question why the Roswell Incident was forgotten so quickly back in 1947. It was buried along with many other wild and fantastic stories.

The Witnesses

The problem with the UFO sightings in 1947 was that there were too many of them. It seemed as if everyone wanted to tell a UFO story. Maybe many of those people just wanted publicity or attention.

The Roswell Incident suffers from this problem. For 30 years it was hardly mentioned—no one made great claims that a UFO and its crew had landed. Then, in 1978, Major Jesse Marcel spoke to investigators, and the story became big news again. Suddenly, after 30 years, witnesses began to come forward with their stories. Too many witnesses to be true!

Following a television program in 1989, even more people claimed to know about the UFO crash and alien bodies. A further 350 witnesses came forward with information—and more are appearing all the time.

Not all of the witnesses are reliable. One woman said that her father had actually performed the autopsy on the little gray men—but her family admitted she had a rather disturbed mind and a very lively imagination. Her father was not even a doctor!

Look at some of the witnesses and their statements and make up your own mind.

MAJOR JESSE MARCEL

In 1978 when interest in UFOs was

reviving, an investigator was told, "Talk to Jesse Marcel." The investigator called Marcel and eventually the incredible story of Marcel's find unfolded. There was even a second witness—Marcel's son, Jesse, Jr., who remembered his father bringing home samples of the wreckage from the crash site. Marcel's evidence became the focus of a large-scale examination of the Roswell Incident. His son described his father's handling of the material:

When Dad came back to the house he had a bunch of wreckage with him at the time and he brought the wreckage into the house. He actually awakened my mother and myself so we could view this, because it was so unusual. This was about two o'clock in the morning as I recall, and he spread it out so we could get some basic idea of what it looked like. We were all amazed by this debris that was there, primarily because we didn't know what it was, you know, it was just the Unknown. Years after this incident happened we would talk privately among ourselves about what this thing was. I know that we came to the conclusion it was not of earthly origin.

BUT:

Jesse Marcel, Sr. could not remember the date of the crash at first. He could not even remember the year! He said it was "sometime toward the end of the 1940s." Perhaps Marcel had a terrible memory—in which case we should doubt everything that he said. Or perhaps the find was so unimportant that Marcel didn't make much of it at the time—in which case he has "invented" new details to make it sensational 30 years later. Ask yourself, if you found foil that couldn't be torn or creased, metal that couldn't be cut or dented, if you had been told to lie about a weather balloon and appear in the newspapers holding up the fake balloon evidence, or would you remember exactly when it happened?

WILLIAM "MAC" BRAZEL

Mac Brazel (pronounce it to rhyme with "dazzle") was the rancher who found the wreckage on his land originally. Throughout his life he refused to talk about what happened. He was especially secretive about the week when he was held in custody by the military authorities. A week in which he started by going on record to say he'd found something odd—and ended by saying he'd found something harmless. His original story was that he'd found pieces of strange metal that couldn't be cut or burned. After he was released, he called the radio station and said:

We haven't got this story right.

Now he was saying he'd found:

Tinfoil, paper, tape, and sticks—the whole thing weighing about five and a half pounds. There was no sign of any metal in the area although at least one paper fin had been glued onto the tinfoil. There were no words to be found anywhere on the instrument although there were some letters on some of the parts. A lot

of Scotch tape (and some tape with flowers printed on it) had been used in the construction. No strings or wires were to be found.

It seems that Mac Brazel also saw the aliens! Before changing his story, he remarked to the radio station owner:

Forget the stories about little green men. They aren't green!

In later years his son, William Brazel, Jr. said that he too had seen the wreckage:

It was something like tinfoil, except it wouldn't tear. You could wrinkle it and lay it back down and it would resume its original shape, almost like plastic but definitely metallic. Dad once said that the army had told him it was nothing made by us. There was also some threadlike material. It looked like silk but it was not silk. A very strong material but without the strands or fibers that silk would have. And there were some woodlike particles, like balsa wood in weight but a bit darker in color and much harder. All I had were a few small bits, but Dad did say one time there were what he called "figures" on some of the pieces he found.

BUT:

How can we explain the huge differences between the stories of the father and the son? One of them must be lying. Mac Brazel could have lied because he was threatened and bribed. William Brazel was young at the time and could have been mistaken about what he saw.

The final proof would have been for modern

scientists to examine the material. Unfortunately, Mac Brazel handed the pieces of metal he had found in the wreckage over to the Counter Intelligence Corps. It is strange that none of the witnesses seem to have hidden even one scrap of the magical metal foil from the forces—or if they did, it has never been found.

Mac Brazel died in 1965 before the story became the subject of popular investigation.

SHERIFF GEORGE A. WILCOX

Sheriff Wilcox was the second person to see samples of the wreckage when Mac Brazel took pieces in for him to look at. Sheriff Wilcox was threatened with death—and the death of his family—if he ever talked. He never did talk publicly and died long before the Roswell Incident became a public sensation. However, his granddaughter spent a lot of time with George Wilcox's wife, Mrs. Inez Wilcox, and she told a remarkable story. She said:

Your grandfather went out to the crash site and there was a big burned area and he saw debris. It was in the evening. There were four space beings. Their heads were large. They wore suits like silk. One of the little men was alive.

BUT:

No one was allowed to see the crash site. If the military was warning George to keep quiet, why would they take him out to show him the place where the craft crashed?

Another problem is that this is the only report that mentions a "burned area" at the Roswell crash site. It suggests that the wreckage site was the same as the site where the aliens were found, whereas other reports agree they were two miles or more apart. Lastly, this is one of the few reports to mention a living alien. Most of the reports agree that the four bodies were dead, or apparently dead, when they were found. Does this sound like a mixture of fact and fairy tale?

CAPTAIN OLIVER HENDERSON

Captain Henderson was supposedly the pilot who transported the alien bodies to the hospital for examination and autopsy. He died in 1986, before investigators could interview him. His accounts have been handed down from friends and family.

In later life Henderson's best friend was a fellow retired officer and dentist, John Kromschroeder. It seems Henderson told Kromschroeder about the wreckage and the aliens as early as 1977. Kromschroeder kept quiet about the story until 1990 when he admitted that he had seen and handled the strange metal from the wreckage.

Investigators believe that the scrap of metal may be among the belongings of the dead pilot. His wife refuses to let them make a search.

Henderson's widow, Sappho, says:

In 1980 or '81 Oliver picked up a newspaper

at a grocery store where we were living in San Diego. One article described the crash of a UFO outside Roswell with the bodies of aliens discovered beside the craft. He pointed out the article to me and said, "I want you to read that article, because it's a true story. I'm the pilot who flew the wreckage of the UFO to Wright Patterson in Dayton, Ohio. I guess now that they've put it in the paper I can tell you about it. I've been wanting to tell you for years." He described the beings as small with large heads for their size. He said the material their suits were made of was like nothing he had ever seen.

He showed the article to his daughter. Later, she said:

When I was growing up we would often spend evenings looking up at the stars. Once I asked him what he was looking for and he said, "I am looking for flying saucers. They're real, you know."

BUT:

These are things the witnesses reported that Henderson had said. The witnesses could have been lying, or Henderson himself could have been making up the stories. Why did Kromschroeder keep quiet until 1990, for example? The family says that Henderson kept his secret from them for 35 years and only felt free to talk when he saw an article about it in the newspaper. Yet he had supposedly revealed it to a friend outside the family five years before—and showed him the scrap of metal. Why didn't the pilot show the metal to his family? Isn't it possible that the newspaper article gave Henderson the opportunity to invent the whole thing rather than the freedom to reveal a true happening?

LIEUTENANT COLONEL ARTHUR EXON— WRIGHT-PATTERSON AIR FORCE BASE

Most reports agree that the wreckage from the crash and the alien bodies were taken to Wright-Patterson Air Force Base in Dayton, Ohio. Arthur Exon was at the base in July 1947 when the wreckage was brought in. He never saw alien bodies but he worked with the people who did. He is certain that the wreckage, the photographs, and the reports are still filed at Wright-Patterson—filed and locked away as "Classified." As for the material itself he said: **We heard the material was coming to Wright Field for testing. Everything from chemical analysis, stress tests, compression tests, flexing. It was brought into our material evaluation labs. I don't know how it arrived but the boys who tested it said it was very unusual. Some of it could be easily ripped, but there were other parts that were very thin but awfully strong and couldn't be dented with heavy hammers. It had them pretty puzzled. They knew they had something new in their hands. The metal and material was unknown to anyone I talked to. A couple of the guys thought it might be Russian, but the overall feeling was that it came from space.** Lieutenant Colonel Exon went on to become a general and a highly respected member of the

U.S. military establishment.

BUT:

Lieutenant Colonel Exon also said:

Whatever the tests found, I never discovered what the results were.

And he never saw the bodies himself. Again it was rumor:

They did say there were bodies. They were all found outside the craft itself but were in fairly good condition.

So, even if this highly respectable General was telling the truth, he is only repeating gossip that he heard over 40 years before. He never saw the results of the test or the autopsy. Both could have offered natural explanations for the crash wreckage and bodies.

THE UFO SPOTTERS

The 1947 sightings are confused because it was a new phenomenon. Not many people knew what to do if they saw something unexplained. Since then ufologists have tried to make spotting a UFO more scientific. They offer the following advice to people who see a UFO:

1 Get as many other witnesses as you possibly can. Write down their names and addresses so they can be contacted later.

2 Make a visual record. If you do have a camera handy then take as many pictures as you can. The background and the foreground are important too because they help to give a "scale" to figure out the size of the unidentified object.

3 Make a written record. Immediately after the sighting, write down everything you saw. Include as much detail as possible. Be sure to include the appearance of the object, its color, its size, and its motion. It is also quite important to write down what you were thinking and feeling when you experienced the sighting.

4 Make note of the location. Mark exactly where you were positioned at the time of the sighting. If the object landed then do what you can to protect that area but do not disturb it. Again, photographs and witnesses to the landing location are important whenever possible.

5 Report it. If you are quite sure that you have seen something unexplained then you could call your nearest police station to report it. They may in turn put you in touch with the nearest center for UFO studies. Calling the local newspaper and having the story published may encourage other people to come forward to confirm they saw the same thing at the same time.

THE DISINFORMATION GAME

If something strange and frightening happened at Roswell, then would the government really have tried to cover the facts up? And if they had, how would they have gone about it?

They could have made the military swear an oath of secrecy, they might have bribed civilians like Mac Brazel, and they might have threatened local officials like Sheriff George Wilcox. But they could also do something much smarter.

They could give researchers information that appears to support the event. The researchers would obviously jump at the information and publish it. At last the UFO world would have the chance to prove that there *was* a strange occurrence at Roswell.

This would create massive public interest—people would look carefully at this exciting new discovery. Then someone notices something that seems to show it is a fake. The public feel cheated and refuses to believe anything about Roswell. The Roswell Incident is forgotten again and the government's secret is safe.

Is that what happened with the M-J 12 documents? And is it what happened with the film of the alien autopsy?

M-J 12

 In 1984 a U.S. movie producer, Jaime Shandera, received a roll of 35mm film.

It had not been developed. He had it developed —and it was sensational. It was a photographed copy of a report code-named "Operation Majestic 12." The report was a note to the President about the discovery, recovery, and analysis of a craft that crashed north of Roswell, New Mexico.

The documents were dated 1952 and included the confirmation that UFO researchers had been looking for:

A local rancher reported the crash of a flying disk-shaped object. On July 7, 1947, a secret operation was begun to assure the recovery of the wreckage of this object for scientific study. During the course of this operation, aerial reconnaissance discovered that four small humanlike beings had apparently ejected from the craft sometime before it exploded. These had fallen to the earth about two miles east of the wreckage site. A special scientific team took charge of removing these bodies for study. News reporters in the area were given the effective cover story that the object had been a misguided weather research balloon.

On the question of the alien bodies the report says:

An analysis of the four dead occupants was arranged by a Dr. Bronk. It was the tentative conclusion of this group (November 30, 1947) that although these creatures are humanlike in appearance, the biological and evolutionary processes responsible for their development have apparently been quite different from those observed in human beings. Dr. Bronk's

team has suggested the term "Extraterrestrial Biological Entities," or "EBEs," be adopted as the standard term of reference for these creatures until such time as a more definitive definition can be agreed on.

As for the power unit of the flying saucer wreckage, the document says:

Efforts to determine the method of propulsion have been unsuccessful. There is a complete absence of identifiable wings, propellers, jets, or other conventional methods of propulsion. There is a total lack of metallic wiring, vacuum tubes, or similar recognizable electronic components. It is assumed that the propulsion unit was completely destroyed by the explosion that caused the crash.

BUT:

Experts say the language in the documents is unlike the language used in 1952; the type style of the lettering is wrong; and of course it's impossible to test the paper and ink of the M-J 12 documents to find out their age because there *are* no documents—only photographs of documents.

The documents also fail to explain what happened to the wreckage and the bodies after they had been examined—surely the President would want to know? And it's a bit too convenient to say the "propulsion unit was destroyed in the crash." If the propulsion unit had *not* been destroyed then the U.S. government would have the secret of intergalactic travel. It hasn't. So, if these documents are fakes then they have to explain *why* there is no power unit.

"Destroyed in the crash" is an easy explanation.

Just ask yourself. A power unit can move the saucers at thousands of miles an hour. How can it be so delicate that it disintegrates in a simple crash that leaves the crew intact?

THE ALIEN AUTOPSY (*see* THE AUTOPSY FOOTAGE *on page 89)*

Ray Santilli is the managing director of the Merlin Group, video-distributors based in London. At some time, Mr. Santilli went across to the United States to get some very old film of Elvis Presley performing on stage—said to be the earliest-ever recording of the dead pop star. While Mr. Santilli was there, an old cameraman (whose name wasn't given) said that he also had some unusual film of an autopsy on an alien corpse, recovered after a UFO crash at Roswell in 1947. Mr. Santilli himself says:

My impression of the cameraman is that he is totally genuine. He is an ordinary person who never really made a great deal of money in his life, has been married to the same woman for over 50 years and seems as stable as anyone could wish. I had the opportunity of going over his many old photo albums, his film collection, and personal papers. I am certain that cameraman was everything he claims. I came away with 22 reels of film.

Mr. Santilli bought the 1947 film for about $150,000, returned to London and copied it onto video, planning to sell it to television companies around the world. He promised to allow experts to see the original old film so they could test that it's the right age and type to have been used in 1947—but he has so far found excuses for not doing this. The film has to be judged from watching the video.

The video is silent and the quality very poor and "grainy" so details cannot be made out even when the tape is freeze-framed.

It shows a humanoid figure—two arms, two legs, two eyes, a mouth, tiny ears and nose, and large, deep-set eyes. Its abdomen is swollen and one leg is seriously damaged as if it has had an accident. The chief nonhuman feature is that it has five fingers plus a thumb on each hand and foot. There is no hair anywhere.

It appears to be lying on a mortuary slab in a white-walled room—perhaps a hospital—while two men in surgical masks conduct an autopsy.

First the dark eyes are removed, or rather a dark film covering white eyeballs. The body is cut open and various organs removed and placed in bowls of liquid—presumably to preserve them. The head is cut open and the skull sawn through to get to the brain. The video is now for sale after being shown to television audiences, but the video sellers are careful to make the following points:

1 The video was made from film manufactured in 1947, but there is no guarantee it was shot in 1947.

2 There are medical reports that suggest that the body is not human but this cannot yet be verified.

3 It is supposed to show the Roswell Incident though this has not been verified.

4 It is not of very clear quality.

BUT:

If ufologists were hoping that the Roswell Autopsy film would show the world that aliens landed and were examined in New Mexico in 1947 then they have been very disappointed. The press reviews of the television showing all agreed it was a hoax:

When you eliminate aircraft, balloons, the planet Venus, lunatics and liars, and other conventional explanations, what you will be left with is nothing.

Sunday Telegraph August 20, 1995.

Serious ufologists were being branded "Lunatics and liars." Other reporters considered them to be simply a joke:

Tonight we are not going to see a cosmic marvel but a fairground attraction on a par with the Amazing Dancing Chickens that "Colonel" Tom Parker toured country fairs in America. The chickens were allegedly taught the balletic art by placing an invisible hot

plate under their feet.
The Daily Telegraph August 28, 1995.

Other newspapers scoffed that the film was
something that belongs in the world of
science fiction and fantasy:
**A four-foot humanoid with a bald head? Pah!
With 12 fingers and 12 toes? Welcome to the
Twilight Zone.**
Daily Mail August 28, 1995.

One of the cruelest reviews came in the
highly respected *Times*...
**Lunatics come in all shapes and sizes. Believe
this and you must be from another planet.**
The Times August 21, 1995.

The one British newspaper to take the film
seriously (*The Sunday People* August 20,
1995) did the Roswell believers no good
either. They claimed that the corpses were
real—

BUT:
**I understand they were connected with germ
warfare and the bodies were of humans who
died following experiments.**
The movie-making experts, who were used to
creating special effects, were no kinder. They
looked at the film closely and declared it was
a fake.
Experts at Pinewood movie studios said they
found the body of the alien was really "a
very good fake body." But special effects
experts could see evidence of a seam down
one arm, suggesting the creature was a

lifelike model. They also picked out the words "Video TV" on parts of the wreckage claimed to be from the crashed flying saucer. Cliff Wallace of the special effects company *Creature Effects* at Pinewood said:

This film is a fake, no doubt about it. It was done very cleverly, probably within our profession, and there is no possibility that it could have been filmed in 1947.
Sheffield Daily Star August 18, 1995.

Others, less expert, could not believe what they saw and guessed at how the fake was constructed:

There is not the slightest reason to believe that this film portrays an autopsy being performed on an alien. Not once, during its whole flickering length, does it contain anything that could reasonably be described as evidence, or could not be put together by a film special-effects department. Various organs were dropped into bowls of preserving fluid. Is it possible that spacemen's flesh and human flesh can be preserved by the same chemical? Or did clever U.S. scientists invent some special substance that prevented the alien bits and pieces from rotting away? All I saw in the grainy, lumpy film was the constant removal of what looked like a pound and a half of calves liver fresh from the butcher's counter. Perhaps the message reaching us from the far end of the universe is that there's a fortune to be made out of space. Let us hope that no one makes one out of the Roswell footage. It is far too silly to be

taken seriously and ought to be laughed all the way back to America.
Daily Mail August 21, 1995.

Other reporters pointed out that a lot of money was to be made out of this sort of fake. The Glasgow *Evening Times* reported on July 8, 1995:
Mr. Santilli is quite clear about his motives—he wants to make money from the film. He said, "Of course it is in my interests not to have the film examined by the UFO community and they are complaining about that. Commercially it suits me to keep the mystery going."
In other words, the more that people argue about the film, the more people will buy it to see for themselves. The UFO believers were quite distressed at the way their beliefs had become a public joke. Expert Don Schmitt said angrily:
This film has nothing to do with Roswell.
While a *UFO Magazine* reader complained:
There was no doubt in my mind the film was a complete farce. If it proves to be a hoax then it could do untold damage to the credibility of Ufology.
Damage the credibility of Ufology? Maybe that's what the U.S. government wanted. If so, they could hardly have done better than make the fake Alien Autopsy film themselves. Perhaps they did!

EXPLANATIONS

Something happened at Roswell in early July 1947. Everyone agrees about that. It appeared in local newspapers and they can be checked. What can't be agreed on is exactly *what* happened. If it wasn't an alien spacecraft accident, then just what was it? What other explanation fits most of the facts? Here are some ideas that have been suggested:

WEATHER BALLOON

This is the story that the air force broadcast, and it could just be true. The balloon landed on the range, and as the wind dragged it across the rough grass and yucca plants, it was shredded so badly that even U.S. Air Force Major, Jesse Marcel could not recognize it. He'd heard all the UFO reports in the press. Rancher Mac Brazel had heard them too, and he wanted the media's $3,000 reward for finding the first UFO. Maybe Brazel tricked Marcel into believing this was alien wreckage. Maybe Brazel even threw in a few "extra" pieces of junk to confuse Marcel and the air force. Maybe that's why the military released a press report saying they'd found a saucer. And maybe that's why Brazel was held in custody and threatened for a week—he'd lied and made the air force look stupid. There was no mystery and no coverup. Thirty years later, people wanting a little bit of publicity—to get their names in the newspapers—came forward with invented stories of little gray men. After 30 years it was hard for them to prove their stories. But it's equally hard to prove that they were liars!

TEST ROCKET

White Sands rocket testing ground is less than 100 miles from Roswell. The Americans were racing against the Russians to develop rocket-powered missiles. The German forces had them by the end of World War II and had caused terror in London with the V-2 flying bombs. The American forces had atom bombs at the end of World War II that had destroyed Japanese cities. Put the two together and they had the most terrible weapon ever invented—a flying atom bomb. This horrific invention would have been the greatest secret in the United States. Development would have involved attaching a nuclear warhead to a captured V-2 and aiming it at a test site. But, if that rocket misfired—and well into the space age 1980s, launches were still going disastrously wrong—then it could crash outside the White Sands test site, 100 miles outside on the plains near Roswell. The nuclear warhead was not "primed" to go off, but it was fitted for test purposes. An air force major would not recognize the disintegrated wreckage—and original German writing on the V-2 rocket was confusing. Meanwhile White Sands was desperately looking for their missing rocket.

When they heard the Roswell press release they swamped the air base and the crash site with security and secrecy—witnesses were either threatened, persuaded, or sworn to secrecy, and a huge cleanup operation was organized. Little gray aliens never existed but may have been invented later by an embarrassed government to distract Americans from what really happened—a very close escape from the world's first nuclear disaster!

SPACE ROCKET

The Americans had no sooner ended the war than they began a space exploration program. This could have had military purposes—the first country to have a weapon base on the Moon could look down on Earth and easily target an enemy. The rockets for space travel would be based on the German V-2s and built by German scientists who had been captured at the end of the war. V-2s were known to have been tested at White Sands. The real problem was that there was very little research into the effects of space travel on the human body. What would happen to the body under the enormous forces of takeoff, the speed of the rocket, and its low-pressure problems at altitude? So the rocket scientists used monkeys in thin, gray thermal suits. As with the test rocket theory, they were forced to cover up their failure when Brazel and Marcel discovered the wreckage. The monkey bodies were spotted and taken back to Wright-Patterson Air Base for examination, where mortician Glenn Dennis was consulted on their preservation but thrown out of the autopsy building. Another possibility is that they were not monkeys but the first men in space. The continuing secrecy and disinformation is because the government does not want to admit to killing four brave test pilots with a clumsy experiment.

JAPANESE BOMB BALLOON

Toward the end of World War II, the Japanese launched over 9,000 balloons with high-explosive bombs attached. They were released and allowed to drift across the Pacific to land on North America. A few actually got through and started small fires. One even killed some people who became too inquisitive when they came across it in the woods. The balloons were larger than the U.S. weather balloons and made from laminated paper or rubberized silk. One could have landed on the ranch and lain there for two years while Mac Brazel could not be bothered to clear the wreckage away. When the UFO scare started, Mac Brazel decided to announce that he had found a saucer and led the military to the bomb balloon. Of course Major Jesse Marcel did not recognize it...but the superior officers in Washington did. They ordered a coverup because they did not want people to think there were dozens of these dangerous devices lying around the plains of America.

U.S. SECRET WEAPON

Mac Brazel said that he heard a crash during a thunder storm on July 2, 1947. It is always possible that the lightning destroyed not an alien craft but a top-secret American war plane. Such a plane would be tested in the emptiest skies the air force could find—over the plains of New Mexico. The airplane would be so secret that ordinary air personnel like Major Jesse Marcel would never have seen one or even known that it existed. No one at the air base of Roswell had ever seen anything like it, so they innocently announced they had found an unidentified flying object—which they had! Just three months after the Roswell wreckage was found, the United States announced that its secret rocket plane the Bell X-1 had flown faster than any airplane before—faster than the speed of sound. A Bell X-1 must have been tested in early July. Perhaps it crashed in the storm and was secretly recovered by the worried Pentagon. The charred and disfigured bodies of the crew may have been found two miles from the main wreckage and taken back to Wright-Patterson for examination and secret burial. They would scarcely be recognizable as human, and rumors of aliens could have arisen from that. These rumors may have been encouraged by a government who didn't want the public to know the true cost of the Bell X-1 success.

RUSSIAN SECRET WEAPON

For 50 years since World War II the United States had been afraid that Russia would get ahead in weapon technology. The Russians had captured German rocket scientists just as the Americans had and were working on guided missile systems and space exploration vehicles too. It is unlikely that the Russians would fly experimentally over the United States, and a rocket so far from Russia was unlikely to be a stray—unless it was very lost indeed. We now know that the Russian rocket experiments were not so advanced in 1947, and they could not have created one that would fly so far. However, in 1947 the American people *thought* the Russians were capable of almost anything. The Roswell wreckage was almost certainly not a Russian secret weapon—but it's possible, in the confusion of finding something odd in the wilds of New Mexico, the Counter Intelligence Corps believed they had found a Russian secret. This accounts for the secrecy, the threats, and the original coverup. It does not explain the continuing 50-year coverup.

ALIEN CRASH LANDING

Maybe none of the above explanations are true. Maybe a flying saucer from another planet really *did* crash land at Roswell.
What do you think?

EPILOGUE

After 50 years it is becoming harder and harder to find positive proof that an alien spacecraft cashed at Corona, near Roswell in New Mexico, or that its alien crew was discovered.

It makes a fascinating story. Unfortunately that is what it could be—just a story. Suppose every human witness was a liar. Is there anything in the classified secret files that could show something very strange crashed at Roswell?

There is. The U.S. Freedom of Information Act has released some reports that were previously secret. Look at them now and something very interesting emerges.

Were there really flying saucers over Earth in 1947? A U.S. army air force report was written in July 1947, when the great UFO scare was at its height. It said:

This "flying saucer" situation is not at all imaginary, or seeing too much in some natural phenomena. Something is really flying around.

This sort of report was never released to the public at that time since it may have caused panic. It became just another government classified report.

Then, in October 1947, an order went out to intelligence agents throughout the world to collect information on the "flying saucer" mystery.

In the orders there was a strange amount of detail. Agents were told to look out for:

Craft constructed from metallic foils and perhaps balsa wood or a similar material

- Unusual construction methods to achieve extreme light weight with structural strength

- Designs with retractable domes to provide for pilot and crew members

- Power sources that are unlike the familiar type of engine and lack fuel systems and fuel storage space

- Power plants that would be part of the craft, not distinguishable as a separate part of the machine

Metallic foils and balsa wood were mentioned by Mac Brazel—after he had examined the wreckage.

Extremely light but strong materials were reported to Lieutenant Colonel Exon when the wreckage was analyzed at the Wright-Patterson Air Base—after they had examined the wreckage.

A separate crew dome was reported by Pilot Oliver Henderson—after he had spotted the second crash site.

The fact that no separate "engine" was found was stated by Major Jesse Marcel—after the first crash site had been searched.

If you see a UFO speeding across the sky

then you don't say, "That's made of metal foil and balsa, it has a separate crew compartment, but no separate fuel tank or power source." How did the government know all these things unless someone had actually examined the remains of a damaged craft? Unless there really *was* a UFO crash at Roswell?

Where is that wreckage now? And were alien corpses really found? We will never know the final answers to the last two questions until a file is opened that has held its secrets secure for 50 years. Until the government releases all the classified files, the final truth about Roswell remains a mystery.

AFTERWORD
THE AUTOPSY FOOTAGE

by Robert Irving

As with all UFO and alien stories, the facts are hard to find. The Roswell autopsy footage is proving to be equally problematic. Having established there were few clues to be found within the film itself, and the fact that most people believe it to be a fake, investigators are now concentrating their efforts on trying to answer perhaps the two most important questions of all: Who made it and why?

This is where I come in. The editor asked me, as a prime suspect for having made the film, for my thoughts, or indeed answers to these questions. I'm not going to provide the answers but I will put forward some further insights.

First, it seems virtually impossible for Ray Santilli to have acquired the film footage from the cameraman we can now identify as Jack Barnett. He died in 1967, age 61. Confronted with this revelation, Ray Santilli now maintains that he is trying to protect the "real" cameraman's identity.

Second, I believe there is a connection between the M-J 12 documents and the film. In fact until those papers emerged, few had heard of Roswell the town—even fewer, the Roswell Incident. Since the autopsy footage was released, the story has hit the headlines. Whether or not the film's content is authentic, the fact remains that something extraordinary *did* happen.

Third, as mentioned in an earlier chapter, the possibility exists that this "evidence" was introduced to us by the very people who have maintained the secret for so long.

Finally, the one-time British government spokesperson on UFOs, ex-Secretariat Air Staff-2A Officer Nick Pope, said of the autopsy footage: **It will be easy to establish the film is a fake, but extremely difficult to prove that it's genuine.** More than one year later, the former has not proven to be *so* easy. So, as we grow more aware that something extraordinary occurred in an isolated New Mexican desert half a century ago—something we weren't meant to know about—we might need to contemplate the notion that this amazing story, even the film footage, could actually be real.